GUARDIANS OF THE HOME
Women's Lives in the 1800s

DAILY LIFE IN AMERICA IN THE 1800s

GUARDIANS OF THE HOME
Women's Lives in the 1800s

by

Matthew Strange

Mason Crest Publishers

MASON CREST PUBLISHERS INC.
370 Reed Road
Broomall, Pennsylvania 19008
(866)MCP-BOOK (toll free)
www.masoncrest.com

First Printing
9 8 7 6 5 4 3 2 1

Library of Congress Cataloging-in-Publication Data

Strange, Matthew.
  Guardians of the home : women's lives in the 1800s / by Matthew Strange.
      p. cm. — (Daily life in america in the 1800s)
  ISBN 978-1-4222-1780-1 (hardcover)   ISBN (series) 978-1-4222-1774-0
  ISBN 978-1-4222-1853-2 (pbk.)   ISBN (pbk. series) 978-1-4222-1847-1
  1. Women—United States—History—19th century—Juvenile literature. 2. Women—United States—Social conditions—19th century—Juvenile literature. I. Title.
  HQ1418.S73 2011
  305.40973'09034—dc22
                                        2010024701
Produced by Harding House Publishing Service, Inc.
www.hardinghousepages.com
Interior Design by MK Bassett-Harvey.
Cover design by Torque Advertising + Design.
Printed in USA by Bang Printing.

Contents

Introduction

History can too often seem a parade of distant figures whose lives have no connection to our own. It need not be this way, for if we explore the history of the games people play, the food they eat, the ways they transport themselves, how they worship and go to war—activities common to all generations—we close the gap between past and present. Since the 1960s, historians have learned vast amounts about daily life in earlier periods. This superb series brings us the fruits of that research, thereby making meaningful the lives of those who have gone before.

The authors' vivid, fascinating descriptions invite young readers to journey into a past that is simultaneously strange and familiar. The 1800s were different, but, because they experienced the beginnings of the same baffling modernity were are still dealing with today, they are also similar. This was the moment when millennia of agrarian existence gave way to a new urban, industrial era. Many of the things we take for granted, such as speed of transportation and communication, bewildered those who were the first to behold the steam train and the telegraph. Young readers will be interested to learn that growing up then was no less confusing and difficult then than it is now, that people were no more in agreement on matters of religion, marriage, and family then than they are now.

We are still working through the problems of modernity, such as environmental degradation, that people in the nineteenth century experienced for the first time. Because they met the challenges with admirable ingenuity, we can learn much from them. They left behind a treasure trove of alternative living arrangements, cultures, entertainments, technologies, even diets that are even more relevant today. Students cannot help but be intrigued, not just by the technological ingenuity of those times, but by the courage of people who forged new frontiers, experimented with ideas and social arrangements. They will be surprised by the degree to which young people were engaged in the great events of the time, and how women joined men in the great adventures of the day.

When history is viewed, as it is here, from the bottom up, it becomes clear just how much modern America owes to the genius of ordinary people, to the labor of slaves and immigrants, to women as well as men, to both young people and adults. Focused on home and family life, books in this series provide insight into how much of history is made within the intimate spaces of private life rather than in the remote precincts of public power. The 1800s were the era of the self-made man and women, but also of the self-made communities. The past offers us a plethora of heroes and heroines together with examples of extraordinary collective action from the Underground Railway to the creation of the American trade union movement. There is scarcely an immigrant or ethic organization in America today that does not trace its origins to the nineteenth century.

This series is exceptionally well illustrated. Students will be fascinated by the images of both rural and urban life; and they will be able to find people their own age in these marvelous depictions of play as well as work. History is best when it engages our imagination, draws us out of our own time into another era, allowing us to return to the present with new perspectives on ourselves. My first engagement with the history of daily life came in sixth grade when my teacher, Mrs. Polster, had us do special projects on the history of the nearby Erie Canal. For the first time, history became real to me. It has remained my passion and my compass ever since.

The value of this series is that it opens up a dialogue with a past that is by no means dead and gone but lives on in every dimension of our daily lives. When history texts focus exclusively on political events, they invariably produce a sense of distance. This series creates the opposite effect by encouraging students to see themselves in the flow of history. In revealing the degree to which people in the past made their own history, students are encouraged to imagine themselves as being history-makers in their own right. The realization that history is not something apart from ourselves, a parade that passes us by, but rather an ongoing pageant in which we are all participants, is both exhilarating and liberating, one that connects our present not just with the past but also to a future we are responsible for shaping.

—*Dr. John Gillis, Rutgers University Professor of History Emeritus*

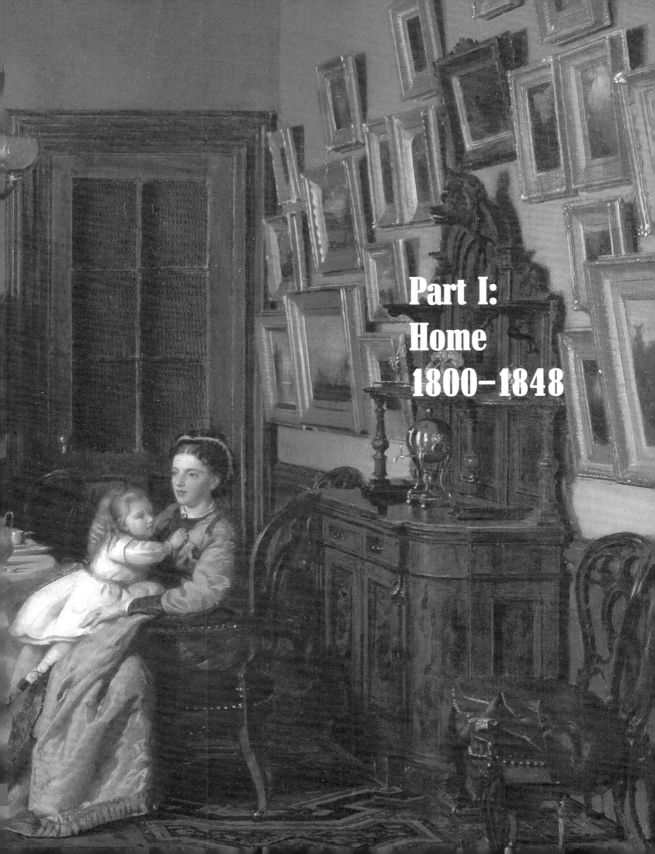

Part I:
Home
1800–1848

1800

1800 The Library of Congress is established.

1800 Abigail Adams becomes the first First Lady to live in the White House when the federal government moves to Washington, D.C.

1801

1801 Thomas Jefferson is elected as the third President of the United States.

1803

1803 Louisiana Purchase—The United States purchases land from France and begins westward exploration.

1812

1812 War of 1812—Fought between the United States and the United Kingdom

1820

1820 Missouri Compromise—Agreement passes between pro-slavery and abolitionist groups, this states that all the Louisiana Purchase territory north of the southern boundary of Missouri (except for Missouri) will be free states, and the territory south of that line will be slave.

1823

1823 Monroe Doctrine—States that any efforts made by Europe to colonize or interfere with land owned by the United States will be viewed as aggression and require military intervention.

1804

1804 Journey of Lewis and Clark—Lewis and Clark lead a team of explorers westward to the Columbia River in Oregon.

1807

1807 Women lose the right to vote in New Jersey, the only state in which they had been able to vote.

1809

1809 Sisters of Charity is founded by Elizabeth Ann Seton in Emmitsburg, Maryland, dedicated to serving the children of the poor.

of the 1800s

1825

1825 The Erie Canal is completed—This allows direct transportation between the Great Lakes and the Atlantic Ocean.

1832

1832 Oberlin College is founded in Ohio. The college admits women and African American students, as well as white men.

1833

1833 The Boston Female Anti-Slavery Society, a women's organization devoted to the abolition of slavery, is founded in Boston, Massachusetts.

Preamble to the Constitution of the Boston Female Anti-Slavery Society.

Believing slavery to be a direct violation of the laws of God, and productive of a vast amount of misery and crime; and convinced that its abolition can only be effected by an acknowledgement of the justice and necessity of *immediate emancipation,*—we hereby agree to form ourselves into a Society TO AID AND ASSIST IN THIS RIGHTEOUS CAUSE AS FAR AS LIES WITHIN OUR POWER.

In some ways nineteenth-century America was very like our world today—but in other ways, it was far different. Imagine a world where mothers didn't work outside the home like fathers, where women were expected to keep quiet and did not have the right to vote, and where a young woman's main objective in life was likely to be to "find a man." We've come so far since those times that it's hard to realize there was a time when men were allowed to play sports and women weren't, or when women were not allowed to go certain places unless accompanied by a man. Today, if you were to tell an American woman she was not allowed to participate in an event, or that she needed to keep her opinions to herself, she'd likely laugh in your face!

Women in the 1800s might not have enjoyed the freedoms women do today, and much about the way they were treated or how they were expected to act might seem unfair (and was!)—but these women behaved strongly and bravely in their own ways, supporting their families, undertaking grueling work, and caring for their children and the men in their lives. The mothers we watch go off to work each morning and the sisters we cheer on at soccer games would not be where they are today had they not stood on the shoulders of the women of the nineteenth century.

During the 1800s, most women spent a great deal of their time caring for children.

Most women in the 1800s spent most of their lives in the home. This was partly because there were limited options for employment outside the home, but the big reason was that the family was the focus of most Americans' lives. Although cities were developing, during the first half of the century the country was still largely rural. Families had to grow their own food, raise their own animals, and make their own clothes. The inside of the home was the woman's domain, while the outside was the man's, and both roles complemented each other. Women might tend to poultry and vegetable gardens, but the men looked after the horses and cattle, and the fields. Men would bring in the cows and clean their stalls; the women might help milk them—and then women would be responsible for making butter and cheese.

Women's Work

A man's work might vary with the seasons, but a woman's work was often almost identical day in and day out. They looked after young children; they cooked; they cleaned the house; and they sewed the family's clothes, washed them, and mended them. A woman's house was her space, her small realm of authority.

You might think of housework as boring or annoying—but you probably don't think it's very physically demanding. Modern inventions like washing machines and vacuum cleaners have made housework far easier. In the 1800s, however, cooking a meal was not as simple as boiling some water over a gas or electric stove or popping something into the microwave. Instead, women had to toil over a coal or wood-burning stove, which were extremely difficult pieces of equipment to use.

In a world with no dishwashers, washing machines, or vacuum cleaners, housework took up much of a woman's day.

First ashes from the previous fire had to be taken out. Then kindling had to be set and the flues (which allow air to flow through the stove, keeping the flames going) had to be adjusted just so. Once the fire was lit, it could not be left unattended. The stove's temperature could not be kept constant without constant attention, and so the woman had to keep a watchful eye on it, even while tending to her other chores, and any time the fire seemed to be going out, she would have to add more wood or coal, or adjust those flues again. Just keeping up with the stove took hours every day.

Preparing the food to be cooked on the stove was even more demanding. Prepared or packaged foods did not come along until much later in the century, so farm animals needed to be butchered and the meat prepared. Bread had to be made, a long process that involved kneading the dough multiple times, then letting it raise. Nuts had to be shelled, jams made, pies baked. Nothing came readymade. Nothing was easy.

Cleaning was as challenging as cooking. The stove produced quantities of smoke, ash, and soot, which meant the entire house—walls, fabrics, tables, and floors—needed frequent cleaning. The menfolk tracked in dirt from the fields. Sweeping, mopping, and beating rugs outdoors were exhausting tasks that had to be done over and over.

Some households, the ones that were wealthy, as well as the emerging urban middle class, hired "help," servants who helped the woman of the household with her work. In the South, before the Civil War, slaves did much of this labor. Even then, however, women and older daughters usually still did some of the work themselves. Few women had much leisure time in their lives. Even when women got together to socialize, they usually quilted or mended at the same time. These quilting and sewing "bees" were rare and special events, however, greatly anticipated as breaks in women's routines. Most of the time, there was just too much to be done for a woman to spend time chatting with a friend.

In the 1800s, many women cooked on stoves similar to this one.

Snapshot from the Past

Diary Entry—a Day Off for Emily
Saturday August 5, 1820

Tomorrow will be wonderful! Mother informed me this past Thursday that I will not be needed to help with the laundry as I do every Monday. After evening church, I am to return home to gather my things, and then Father is going to walk me to the Higgins'. I will stay overnight with Mrs. Higgins, as she is feeling poorly, and I will read to her and help her with the meals. I am very excited to be missing laundry day. There is nothing I detest more. The soap bothers me so and my arms always hurt for days after having to carry the water buckets. Instead, I will be spending most of the day sitting by the fire, reading out loud. I wonder what books Mrs. Higgins has?

The most arduous task for any American housewife in the 1800s was the laundry. Washing the family's clothes took an entire day, if not longer. First, she would soak the clothes in tubs of warm water. Then, she would scrub the laundry on a washboard and rub it with lye soap, which was very irritating to her hands. After that, she would put the clothes in boiling water while stirring them with a large pole. Finally, she would rinse the clothes twice, then wring them out and hang them on clotheslines to dry.

That all sounds bad enough. But now take one more fact into consideration: in the early nineteenth century, indoor plumbing was essentially a dream. Most people in America still got their water by hand from wells or pumps, or even nearby streams. So the 50 gallons or so that the laundry required? Women had to carry it all themselves in buckets.

Housework took up most of the time for the typical American woman in the nineteenth century. To iron the clothes, this young woman would need at least two irons—one to use while the other is heating on the stove. Irons needed to be hot enough to smooth away the wrinkles, but not so hot that they scorched the cloth, and getting the right temperature could be tricky. Irons also needed to be kept very clean and polished so they didn't harm the fabric.

The Other American Women

The tasks of cooking, cleaning, and child care were so basic to women's lives, that in some ways white women's lives weren't all that different from Native and African American women's. The wealthier a white woman was, the more luxuries she was likely to experience, but for most, especially in rural areas and on the frontier, white women were occupied with much the same tasks as Native and African American women. All of them fetched water, prepared and cooked food, made clothing, and raised the children.

than a human being, she also lived a life in which abuse and rape were ever-present possibilities. Even a slave lucky enough to have a kind master was still his property and denied the rights that white women had. Her children or her husband could be sold and sent away from her, and she might never see them again. In states like Virginia, a freed slave had to leave the state or risk being sold into slavery again. Some freed slaves chose this option to be able to remain with spouses, children, or other family members.

Native women, depending on their tribe and where they lived, also helped set up and take down camps. They planted and cultivated food, processed animal hides, and made pots and baskets. In the Southwest, they often spun and wove wool.

A slave woman working in a Southern home had it worse, however, since she would do all these chores for her owners and then probably have to do the same chores in her own home. Since she was considered to be property rather

A black woman and her child do the laundry in a kettle over an open fire.

EYEWITNESS ACCOUNT

Petition of Lucinda to the General Assembly

27 November 1815.

To the Legislature of the Commonwealth of Virginia,

The petition of Lucinda, lately a slave belonging to Mary Matthew of King George county respectfully sheweth. That the said Mary Matthews by her last will and testament, among other things, emancipated all her slaves, and directed that they should be removed by her executor to someplace where they could enjoy their freedom by the laws there in force.

That all the slaves so emancipated (except your petitioner) were removed this year to the State of Tennessee, but your petitioner declined going with them, as she had a husband belonging to Capt: William H. Hooe in King George county, from whom the benefits and privileges to be derived from freedom, dear and flattering as they are, could not induce her to be separated: that, in consequence of this determination on her part, a year has elapsed since the death of her late mistress Mary Matthews, and your petitioner is informed that the forfeiture of her freedom has taken place under the law prohibiting emancipated slaves from remaining in this State; and that the Overseers of the Poor might now proceed to sell her for the benefit of the Poor of the county: Your petitioner, still anxious to remain with her husband, for whom she has relinquished all the advantages of freedom, is apprehensive that, in case of sale of her by the Overseers of the Poor, she may be purchased by some person, who will remove her to a place remote from the residence of her husband: to guard against such a heart-rending circumstance, she would prefer, and hereby declares her consent, to become a slave to the owner of her husband, if

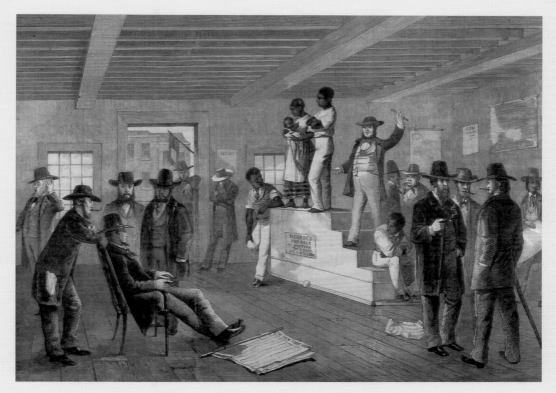

Slaves had no rights to their own families. If their owners decided, husbands and wives, mothers and children, could be taken away from each other and sold separately.

your honorable body will permit it, and for that purpose she prays that you will pass a law vesting the title to her in the said William H. Hooe and directing that all proceedings on the part of the Overseers of the Poor for King George county to effect the sale of her may be perpetually staid;

And your petitioner will pray etc
Lucinda

Women Who Made a Difference

You might think that women would have been so busy with housework that they would have had no opportunities to touch the outside world in any way. And in fact, countless intelligent, talented, and capable women no doubt lived and died with their influence on their husbands and sons the only power they had to shape and change the world.

But even then, some women found ways to reach beyond their culture's expectations of them—women like Harriet Beecher Stowe, whose book *Uncle Tom's Cabin* helped bring about the end of slavery; Dorothea Dix, who

Sojourner Truth

exposed the poor treatment of the mentally ill; Sacajawea, the Shoshone woman who traveled with the Lewis and Clark expedition; and Sojourner Truth, a woman born into slavery who went on to preach about abolition and women's rights—and because of their courage and determination, they brought important changes to America. Meanwhile, ordinary woman kept America fed and clothed and healthy. Without them, America in its youngest years would have fallen apart.

Dorothea Dix

Sacajawea was a young mother with an infant when she helped lead Lewis and Clark across North America.

INCREDIBLE INDIVIDUAL
Harriet Beecher Stowe

Born in 1811 in Litchfield, Connecticut, Harriet Beecher Stowe is mostly remembered for her novel "Uncle Tom's Cabin" about the lives of African Americans under slavery.

Harriet was the daughter of a fiery religious leader, Lyman Beecher, and Roxana Foote, a deeply religious woman who died when Harriet was only four years old. Harriet pursued higher education at a seminary run by her older sister Catharine. A few years later, she moved to Cincinnati, Ohio, to be near her father, who had taken a position there as president of Lane Theological Seminary. There she married Calvin Ellis Stowe, a professor and outspoken opponent of slavery. While living in Ohio, Harriet and Calvin supported the Underground Railroad, a system for secretly helping escaped slaves. Eventually, Harriet and Calvin moved back east to Brunswick, Maine, where he took a position at Bowdoin College and she stayed busy raising their seven children.

It was while living in Brunswick and raising her seven children that Harriet wrote the novel for which she is most remembered today. In 1850, Congress passed the Fugitive Slave Law, stating that it was illegal to assist escaped slaves, and this law prompted her to write "Uncle Tom's Cabin." The book, which was first published in installments in the antislavery journal "National Era," was one of the first pieces of literature to paint the realities of slavery for a national audience. It excited an increase in antislavery attitudes in the North and widespread anger in the South.

The book sold roughly 300,000 copies between 1852 and 1853 alone. It was translated into multiple languages, and had a radical effect on politics in both the United States and Europe. The book was so powerful in the fight against slavery that upon meeting Harriet, Abraham Lincoln is rumored to have said, "So you're the little lady who started this great war!"

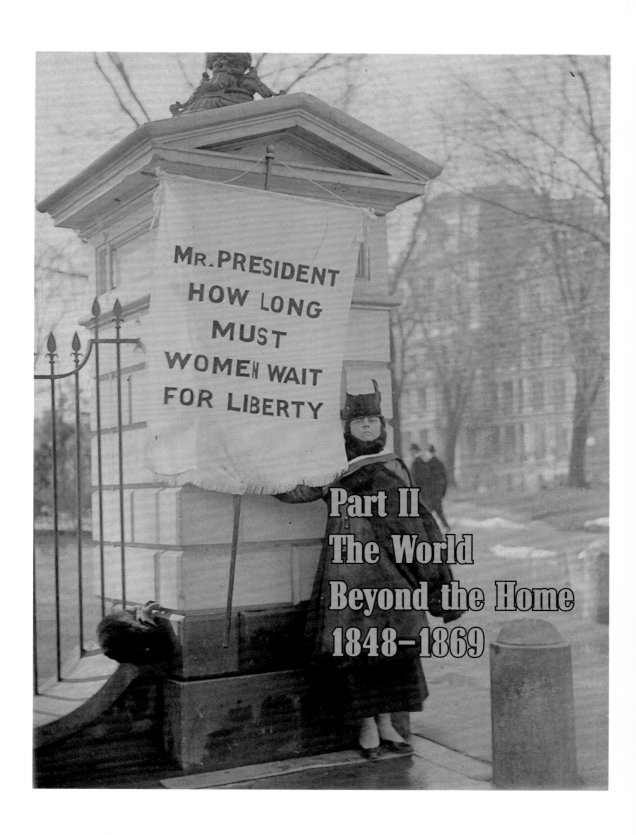

MR. PRESIDENT
HOW LONG
MUST
WOMEN WAIT
FOR LIBERTY

Part II
The World
Beyond the Home
1848–1869

1837

1837 Mary Lyon founds Mount Holyoke Female Seminary, the first women's college in the United States. The school later changed its name to Mount Holyoke College.

1838

1838 Trail of Tears—General Winfield Scott and 7,000 troops force Cherokees to walk from Georgia to a reservation set up for them in Oklahoma (nearly 1,000 miles). Around 4,000 Native Americans die during the journey.

1839

1839 The first camera is patented by Louis Daguerre.

1850

1850 The first National Women's Rights Convention is held in Worcester, Massachusetts.

1854

1854 Kansas-Nebraska Act—States that each new state entering the country will decide for themselves whether or not to allow slavery. This goes directly against the terms agreed upon in the Missouri Compromise of 1820.

1861

1861(-65) Civil War —Fought between the Union and Confederate states.

1844

1844 First public telegraph line in the world is opened—between Baltimore and Washington.

1848

1848 Seneca Falls Convention—Feminist convention held for women's suffrage and equal legal rights.

1848(-58) California Gold Rush—Over 300,000 people flock to California in search of gold.

1849

1849 Elizabeth Blackwell is the first woman to receive a medical degree from Geneva Medical College in Geneva, New York.

of the 1800s

1862

1862 Emancipation Proclamation—Lincoln states that all slaves in Union states are to be freed.

1864

1864 Abolitionist and women's rights activist Sojourner Truth meets President Lincoln.

1865

1865 Thirteenth Amendment to the United States Constitution—Officially abolishes slavery across the country.

1865 President Abraham Lincoln is assassinated on April 15.

Women who were so important to the development of what was considered the foundation of the American community—the family—were not allowed the rights to influence that community. They could not vote or hold public office.

Little girls went to school alongside little boys, but women had little or no access to higher education, and they could not become lawyers, doctors, or clergy. Caring for and teaching young children were considered to be the only occupations outside the home appropriate for women. Legally, a wife essentially did not exist without her husband. A woman could not own property, and in the unlikely event that she and her husband were divorced, she could not gain custody of her children.

But as the century progressed, many things began changing in America, and the role of women was a part of those changes. The first change had stemmed from changes in how children were viewed: instead of being seen as miniature adults, children began to be valued in a new way, along with childhood, and mothers were honored for the important roles they played in shaping their children's lives. Motherhood was no longer merely menial labor; instead, women were expected to teach their children and shape them

The young woman in the center of this picture took advantage of one of the new careers open to women to become responsible for teaching all the children in this school.

morally. As a result, women began to take themselves more seriously. They realized their worth in society.

The first women's colleges were established, offering new opportunities other than marriage to young women.

Many women began to choose to marry later. (In the 1700s and the early part of the 1800s, many girls were married before they were sixteen.) Unmarried women found new employment opportunities in factories and as teachers.

INCREDIBLE INDIVIDUAL
Mary Lyon

Born in Buckland, Massachusetts in 1797, Mary Lyon became a famous educator and religious leader. One of seven children, she attended school until she was thirteen years old, and got her first job as a teacher while she was still in her teens.

She taught and managed other schools in New England before establishing her own in 1837, the first all-women's college in the country—the Mount Holyoke Female Seminary in South Hadley, Massachusetts. Now known as Mount Holyoke College, the school is still in existence today, having carried on Mary Lyon's legacy long after her death in 1849.

If women's influence was so important to society, women began to ask, then what else might women be capable of if they were given the chance? A new movement began to emerge in the 1840s: women's rights. Leaders in this struggle stepped forward, eager to

Catherine Beecher

change the world for the better. Women like Catherine Beecher and Sarah J. Hale lead the fight to persuade school boards to allow women to work as teachers, while they also drew attention to the abysmal wages women earned in industrial jobs. Beecher and Hale challenged the males who ran factories and mills to pay women wages equal to those of men.

The women working in this textile mill were among the first to have the opportunity to earn money away from their homes.

Still, in terms of everyday life, very little was changing. Most families still lived on farms, and women continued to tend to their large households. Slave women on Southern plantations still worked alongside their male counterparts in the field, or they were put to work inside large plantation houses, helping to prepare food for their master and watch after his children.

On the national and political level, very little changed either, at least on the surface. The women's rights movement achieved small victories, in terms of providing some property rights for married women. And women played a role in the growing Abolitionist movement against slavery. Even there, however, while women were allowed to demonstrate support and donate funds,

In the middle of the nineteenth century, most families still lived on farms.

they were barred from many meetings and discussions. At a World Anti-Slavery Convention held in 1840, three American women were chosen as representatives—but when they arrived at the convention they were denied the right to participate and were forced to sit in the balcony.

The Anti-Slavery convention in 1840.

A group of Philadelphia abolitionists.

A group of Philadelphia abolitionists with Lucretia Mott [seated second from the right].

The Growth of the Women's Rights Movement

Eight years later though, that same denial would be the catalyst for the first women's rights convention in history. In July of 1848, Lucretia Mott (one of the female representatives who had not been allowed to participate in the

Elizabeth Cady Stanton

anti-slavery convention eight years earlier) and Elizabeth Cady Stanton met socially with four other women. As they were talking, they had the idea of calling a convention to examine the social and civil rights of women.

By July 20th, just days after that first meeting, Stanton had drafted the Declaration of Sentiments (based on America's Declaration of Independence), and the women held their convention in Seneca Falls, New York, drawing a

Lucretia Mott

THE FIRST CONVENTION

EVER CALLED TO DISCUSS THE

Civil and Political Rights of Women,

SENECA FALLS, N. Y., JULY 19, 20, 1848.

WOMAN'S RIGHTS CONVENTION.

A Convention to discuss the social, civil, and religious condition and rights of woman will be held in the Wesleyan Chapel, at Seneca Falls, N. Y., on Wednesday and Thursday, the 19th and 20th of July current; commencing at 10 o'clock A. M. During the first day the meeting will be exclusively for women, who are earnestly invited to attend. The public generally are invited to be present on the second day, when Lucretia Mott, of Philadelphia, and other ladies and gentlemen, will address the Convention.*

---

*This call was published in the *Seneca County Courier*, July 14, 1848, without any signatures. The movers of this Convention, who drafted the call, the declaration and resolutions were Elizabeth Cady Stanton, Lucretia Mott, Martha C. Wright, Mary Ann McClintock, and Jane C. Hunt.

---

crowd of about 300—about 260 women and 40 or so men. Most people considered the convention to be merely a curiosity; nevertheless, it triggered new conversations across America: Were women being treated fairly? Were women intelligent enough to vote?

It would be another seventy-two years before the Nineteenth Amendment finally did give women the right to vote. Neither Stanton nor Mott would be alive to see that day—but it was their idea that began the revolution.

EXTRA! EXTRA!

From The North Star, Rochester, N.Y.
July 28, 1848

Editorial by Frederick Douglass, written in response to the Women's Rights Convention at Seneca Falls.

We should not do justice to our own convictions, or to the excellent persons connected with this infant movement, if we did not in this connection offer a few remarks on the general subject which the Convention met to consider and the objects they seek to attain. In doing so, we are not insensible that the bare mention of this truly important subject in any other than terms

The Seneca Falls Convention was not the beginning of the women's rights movement, but it was an important event that got people talking. Suffragists were active and visible after that time until women were finally granted the right to vote in 1920.

This political cartoon shows a court of women trying a man for "breach of promise" to a woman, indicating women's growing anger and militancy.

of contemptuous ridicule and scornful disfavor, is likely to excite against us the fury of bigotry and the folly of prejudice. A discussion of the rights of animals would be regarded with far more complacency by many of what are called the wise and the good of our land, than would be a discussion of the rights of women. It is, in their estimation, to be guilty of evil thoughts, to think that a woman is entitled to equal rights with man. Many who have at last made the discovery that the negroes have some rights as well as other members of the human family, have yet to be convinced that women are entitled to any. . . . It is perhaps

Frederick Douglass

Elizabeth Cady Stanton speaking at the convention.

needless to say, that we cherish little sympathy for such prejudices. Standing as we do upon the watch-tower of human freedom, we cannot be deterred from an expression of our approbation of any movement, however humble, to improve and elevate the character of any members of the human family. While it is impossible for us to go into this subject at length, and dispose of the various objections which are often urged against such a doctrine as that of female equality, we are free to say that in

THE AGE OF BRASS.
or the triumphs of Woman's rights

THE AGE OF IRON.

MAN AS HE EXPECTS TO BE

The cartoons on this page and the facing page are an exaggerated look at what men feared might happen if women were allowed to vote and gain the same rights as men.

respect to political rights, we hold woman to be justly entitled to all we claim for man. We go farther, and express [our] conviction that all political rights that it is expedient for man to exercise, it is equally so for woman. All that distinguishes man as an intelligent and accountable being, is equally true of woman; and if that government only is just which governs by the free consent of the governed, there can be no reason in the world for denying to woman the exercise of the elective franchise, or a hand in making and administering the laws of the land. Our doctrine is that "right is of no sex." We therefore bid the women engaged in this movement our humble Godspeed.

INCREDIBLE INDIVIDUAL
Susan B. Anthony

Susan B. Anthony was instrumental in getting women the right to vote. She was born into a Quaker family in 1820, where she was brought up to believe in women's equality. She eventually moved to Rochester, New York, where she joined the temperance movement. In New York, she was inspired by the growing women's rights movement as well, and ended up dedicating her life to that cause. Anthony joined with Elizabeth Cady Stanton, another supporter of women's rights, and together they traveled across the United States to give speeches and inspire others; they also founded the National Woman's Suffrage Association (NWSA) to specifically fight for women's right to vote. Anthony died in 1906, 14 years before women were given the right to vote, but she was able to see the status of women grow over her lifetime.

INCREDIBLE INDIVIDUAL
Lucretia Mott

Lucretia Mott is a less well-known figure than either Susan B. Anthony or Elizabeth Cady Stanton, but was nevertheless a key part of the women's rights movement of the late 1800s. Her interest in women's lack of rights began when she traveled to England to attend a World Anti-Slavery Convention. She and her fellow women delegates—including Stanton—were refused seats because of their sex. Upon returning to the United States, she was the first to sign the Declaration of Sentiments, the product of the Seneca Falls Convention in 1848, and continued to be at the forefront of the women's rights movement until her death in 1880.

The Civil War

Other struggles were going on as well during these years in America. The Civil War tore apart the nation, but despite the War's hardship and suffering, women found new opportunities. Whether from the North or South, women picked up the work of keeping up the home while the men were away. Now, it was not only the inside of the house that was their responsibility; with the men all off to war, women worked the fields and cared for the horses and cows. Women also organized supplies and raised funds to send to soldiers, and they nursed the wounded.

Clara Barton in 1865.

This illustration features images of the important roles that women played in the Civil War. From an original 1862 *Harper's Weekly* newspaper.

The most famous of these women is probably Clara Barton, the founder of the American Red Cross. After the Battle of Bull Run, Barton learned that soldiers were dying needlessly, simply for lack of supplies. She immediately advertised in a local paper, received huge donations, and then set up a distribution agency. For the remainder of the war, she would be known as "the Angel of The Battlefield" for the care she provided the wounded troops. She had seen a need—and she did something about it.

Women on the Frontier

The determination and strong will demonstrated by women like Clara Barton could also be seen in frontier women. These women were generally understood to be of a tougher breed than their Eastern sisters. After coping with the general hardships of the long journey west, women out in the unsettled parts of the country were more likely to work alongside the men, mending fences, helping in the fields, and tending to livestock. This initially was out of necessity, but as women proved themselves, men gradually realized that women were more capable than they had once thought. That is probably part of the reason why Wyoming, a frontier state, was the first to allow women to vote, passing the law in December of 1869, many years ahead of the rest of the nation.

That revolutionary spirit hadn't yet reached the world of fashion. In the mid- to late nineteenth century, men's clothing was beginning to become

Out of necessity, frontier women had to do as much of the heavy labor as men. At times, women might be left alone for weeks or months at a time—or even longer if their husbands died—and they needed to be able to take care of the farm, provide for the family, and protect themselves from any dangers that came along.

looser and somewhat more casual. Women, however, were still expected to wear full and formal dresses. Their long, tight-waisted dresses were not designed to allow them freedom of movement. In fact, women's fashions made sure that women would remain dependent on men in any effort that required physical exertion!

Women's worlds had begun to expand, however—and this expansion, once it had begun, could not be stopped.

Part III
New Opportunities
1869–1900

1867

1867 United States purchases Alaska from Russia.

1868

1868 Susan B. Anthony begins publishing "The Revolution," a weekly journal devoted to women's rights.

1869

1869 Transcontinental Railroad completed on May 10.

1869 Susan B. Anthony and Elizabeth Cady Stanton found the National Woman's Suffrage Association (NWSA), an organization devoted to advocating equal rights for women.

1878

1878 Thomas Edison patents the phonograph on February 19.

1878 Thomas Edison invents the light bulb on October 22.

1881

1881 Clara Barton, who had aided wounded soldiers in the Civil War, founds the American Red Cross.

1886

1886 The Statue of Liberty is dedicated on October 28.

1890

1890 Wounded Knee Massacre— Last battle in the American Indian Wars.

1870

1870 Fifteenth Amendment to the United States Constitution—Prohibits any citizen from being denied to vote based on their "race, color, or previous condition of servitude."

1870 Christmas is declared a national holiday.

1872

1872 Women's rights advocate Susan B. Anthony is arrested for illegally voting in the 1872 presidential election.

1876

1876 Alexander Graham Bell invents the telephone.

1877

1877 Great Railroad Strike—Often considered the country's first nationwide labor strike.

of the 1800s

1892

1892 Ellis Island is opened to receive immigrants coming into New York.

1896

1896 Plessy vs. Ferguson—Supreme Court case that rules that racial segregation is legal as long as accommodations are kept equal.

1896 Henry Ford builds his first combustion-powered vehicle, which he names the Ford Quadricycle.

1896 The National Association of Colored Women is formed, bringing together more than 100 black women's clubs.

1898

1898 The Spanish-American War—The United States gains control of Cuba, Puerto Rico, and the Philippines.

Despite the many new ideas floating around America by the last part of the century, very little had changed for most women. They were still living their lives much as they always had, going about their duties, focusing on the everyday demands and expectations of their homes and communities.

Marriage

Young women during these years were expected to be focused on the task of finding a suitable husband. Although women had begun marrying later, usually between the ages of eighteen and twenty-five (because of an increased focus on schooling, individual employment, and the decision to have fewer children), the process of attracting a man of good background and financial security was as challenging and time consuming as ever.

Nowadays we expect a young woman to go off to college or start a career at age eighteen, form her own identity, have her own dreams and goals, and

pursue (or not pursue if she so chooses) whatever life companion she chooses. But in a world where women still had very few individual rights, expectations were far different. Marriage was the only way women could be financially secure. Unmarried women had no hope of property ownership, and their inclusion in proper society was restricted.

All this made the decision of whom to marry a central focus of young women's lives. Women and their families did not approach the subject lightly. Although a woman may have felt pressure from family to accept a proposal from a specific suitor, in America, then as now, she usually had the option to refuse the proposal.

Once married, children became the next goal for all women. In the eyes of society, a woman's success was based heavily on whether or not she had children —and how she was able to raise them.

Spinsters

Some women did live alone and never married. Their numbers were increasing during the second half of the 1800s, but they were still the minority, and society did not always give them much respect. Referred to as "spinsters," they might not have been seen as outright outcasts, so long as they were employed to mend clothes, care for children, or do other "respectable" jobs to support themselves. The lives of these women were challenging and often lonely. Nevertheless, some women intentionally chose this life rather than give up their independence within marriage. They had

Mary Cassatt (shown in this self-portrait) never married or had children, devoting her life instead to art. Her works focus on the daily lives of women and children, giving glimpses into a world rarely seen in public.

strong wills and the determination to live their lives as they saw fit.

Some women, however, managed to both marry and develop individual skills that set them apart and—in some cases—made them successful and famous.

Louisa May Alcott, author of *Little Women*, and many other books, never married either, although she took in and raised both a niece and a nephew.

INCREDIBLE INDIVIDUAL
Annie Oakley

Annie Oakley was born in Ohio on August 13, 1860. By the time she was nine years old or so, she was shooting local game to help support her poor family. People who knew her soon recognized her amazing sharp-shooting ability, and as she grew older, she was able to create a lucrative career around her talent. After beating Frank E. Butler in a shooting competition, the couple married, with Butler working as Oakley's assistant.

Eventually the two took their act to Buffalo Bill's Wild West Show in 1885, where audiences were treated to Oakley's ability to shoot a hole in a playing card and the ashes off a cigarette.

When Annie died in 1926, the entire nation mourned her. Eventually her life story was retold in the famous musical (1946) *Annie Get Your Gun*.

Working Women

Many women, especially widows, owned businesses by the second half of the nineteenth century. Women worked as storekeepers, barbers, blacksmiths, printers, tavern keepers, and midwives. As the Industrial Revolution took hold in the United States, more women went to work outside the home in factories; by the 1870s, as many as 15 percent of all American women worked outside the home.

Factory owners hired women and children whenever they could, because they could pay them lower wages than they had to pay men. For some tasks, like sewing, women were preferred because they had training and experience—and in men's minds, these jobs were "women's work." The sewing machine was not introduced into the factory system until the 1830s; before that, sewing was done by hand.

Even though wages were often low in textile mills, and conditions could be difficult or even horrible, women took these jobs because they were a way of earning money and taking charge of their own lives. Some women were able to save enough money working in the mills to pay for a college education.

Female employees label cans at LaPorte's Heinz pickle factory. Photo courtesy of LaPorte County Historical Society Museum.

Lowell Mills in Massachusetts was one of the first factories in America to employ many women. Workers spent long hours on their feet surrounded by noisy machines. Yet, the mills were generally clean and orderly.

The company hired young women from farms near the mills. The Lowell girls, as they came to be called, usually sent their wages home to their families. At first, parents hesitated to let their daughters work in the mills, so the company built boardinghouses to make parents feel better about sending their daughters to work. The company also made rules to protect the young women. Companies like Lowell Mills set high standards for quality working conditions. Unfortunately, Lowell would prove to be unusual in the late 1800s, when many factory owners treated their workers poorly.

New Fashions

By the end of the century, women were still expected to wear dresses all the time. Today we usually think of a dress as something women wear when getting "dressed up," but in the 1800s, no women wore pants. Even slave women working in the fields wore dresses. In fact, no matter what they were doing, even if they were playing a sport, women wore dresses. But a new popular leisure activity finally brought a change to women's clothing.

Toward the end of the century, leisure time for everyone had begun to slowly increase. Men may have had more options for their leisure time, but women were not entirely excluded from this movement. Popular activities for women included tennis, croquet—and bicycling. Women managed to wear long skirts while playing croquet and tennis. The thought of a woman sprinting across the court during a tennis match while wearing a full-length dress might seem ridiculous to us, but nineteenth-century women managed to cope with this cultural handicap. Nor did long skirts seriously get in a woman's way while she swung a croquet mallet. Riding a bicycle while

wearing a dress, however, presented more serious problems. The first issue was with "decency." No woman wanted to expose her bare legs, let alone her undergarments. Safety was another concern, since long skirts could easily get caught in the bicycle's gears, causing accidents and possible injuries.

These problems were solved by a new clothing option for the bicycle-riding woman: bloomers. This style usually consisted of a slightly shorter than usual dress with bloomers underneath it, worn with tall laced boots to cover the ankles (so as not to be too revealing).

Bloomers were first introduced in the 1850s, but most people thought they were ridiculous and they didn't catch on. Later in the century, they began to become more popular, especially for use during bicycle riding or playing sports.

Just as today, women's fashions in the 1800s changed from year to year. These drawings show some of the typical dress styles between 1794 and 1887.

"**Morning & Evening dresses; the newest Fashions for May 1829,**" fashion head-lines from a 19th-century woman's magazine.

This revolutionary change in women's clothing was a sign of still greater changes to come in the new century. Women had discovered that they could be independent and competent—and they began to find ways to escape from the restrictions that had held them back for centuries. At the same time, they were trying to balance these newfound feelings of independence and individuality with the expectations and restrictions of nineteenth-century American society.

Still, change had been put in motion, and once started, it could not be stopped. The new century would be an exciting time for women here in America, filled with opportunities born from the new ideas of the 1800s.

Think About It

The women's rights movement that had its roots in the 1800s has had a huge impact on the lives of American women.

Using what you've learned in this book, think about what the life of an average American young woman, about your age, was like in the 1800s and compare it with the life of an average American young woman today.

- What was a normal day for a young woman in the 1800s like? Describe it in as much detail as you can, from the time she gets up in the morning until she goes to bed at night. Do the same for a young woman of today. How are they different? And in what ways are they the same? Which seems more interesting to you?

- What sort of options did a young woman in the 1800s have for her future? What was her life likely to be like in ten years? In forty years? What about today's young woman?

- Do you think the founders of the women's rights movement, women like Elizabeth Cady Stanton, would be satisfied with the progress women have made in the last 150 years? Is there still progress that needs to be made?

Words Used in This Book

abolition: The legal ending of something. In the 1800s the word was used especially to refer to the movement to end slavery.

abysmal: Extremely or hopelessly bad.

catalyst: Something that starts an important change.

complemented: Something improved by being made complete and whole.

frontier: A newly settled area where living conditions are often rough.

grueling: A task that is extremely tiring and demanding.

leisure: Time that is free from the demands of work or duty and can be used for relaxation and enjoyment.

lucrative: Profitable and money-making,

midwives: Women who are trained to assist in the birthing of babies

processed: Changed from an unfinished form to a finished one, like the tanning of an animal hide into leather.

Find Out More

In Books

Burton, Annie. *Women's Slave Narratives*. Mineola, N.Y.: Dover Publications, 2006.

Forman-Brunel, Miriam, Leslie Paris. *The Girls' History and Culture Reader: The Nineteenth Century*. Champaign, Ill.: University of Illinois Press, 2010.

Jabour, Anya. *Scarlett's Sisters: Young Women in the Old South*. Chapel Hill, N.C.: University of North Carolina Press, 2009.

McMillen, Sally Gregory. *Seneca Falls and the Origins of the Women's Rights Movement*. Oxford, U.K.: Oxford University Press, 2008.

On the Internet

Kitchen Gadgets of the 1800s
www.oldandinteresting.com/kitchen-antiques.aspx

Life of the Victorian Woman
www.victoriaspast.com/LifeofVictorianWoman/LifeofVictorianWoman.html

The Lowell Mill Girls Go on Strike
historymatters.gmu.edu/d/5714

Sacajawea
www.lewisandclarktrail.com/sacajawea.html

Women's Rights National Historical Park
www.nps.gov/wori/index.html

Index

Picture Credits

To the best knowledge of the publisher, all images used in this book are in the public domain. If any image has been inadvertently uncredited, please notify Harding House Publishing Service, 220 Front Street, Vestal, New York 13850 so that credit can be given in future printings.

About the Author and the Consultant

Matthew Ronald Strange is a writer living in Richmond, Virginia. He has worked as an editor and as a copywriter, but his true passion is writing creatively: short stories, poetry, and maybe someday a novel. This is his first time writing for Mason Crest.

John Gillis is a Rutgers University Professor of History Emeritus. A graduate of Amherst College and Stanford University, he has taught at Stanford, Princeton, University of California at Berkeley, as well as Rutgers. Gillis is well known for his work in social history, including pioneering studies of age relations, marriage, and family. The author or editor of ten books, he has also been a fellow at both St. Antony's College, Oxford, and Clare Hall, Cambridge.